MR. MELVIN
THE MONEY MASTER
and the Rule of 72

Grow your money as you grow older and wiser

ROGER F. HARTWICH JR. | MSE, MS

Mr. Melvin the Money Master and the Rule of 72: Grow your money as you grow older and wiser

First Print Edition

Copyright @ 2020 RFH-RLP Real Life Publishing, LLC

All rights reserved. No part of this book may be reproduced or transmitted in any form by any means, electronic or mechanical, including photocopying, recording, or by any information storage and retrieval system without the written permission of the author, except where permitted by law.

Disclaimer: This publication contains material primarily for educational and informational purposes. The author and publisher have made earnest effort to ensure that the information in this book was correct at publication time and do not assume, and hereby disclaim, any liability to any party for any loss, damage, or disruption caused by errors and omissions.

Cover and Interior Design by Kendra Cagle, www.5LakesDesign.com

ISBN: 978-1-7362828-0-9

Table of Contents

Preface i

Introduction 1

1. **Savings and Checking Account** 5
2. **Insurance** 9
3. **Taxes** 11
4. **Invest** 13
5. **Individual Retirement Account (IRA)** 17
6. **Interest** 19
7. **Principal** 21
8. **Compounding** 23
9. **Debt** 25
10. **Mortgage** 25
11. **Credit** 27
12. **Rule of 72** 29

Summary/Conclusion 41

Glossary of Terms 45

Worksheets 47

About the Author 56

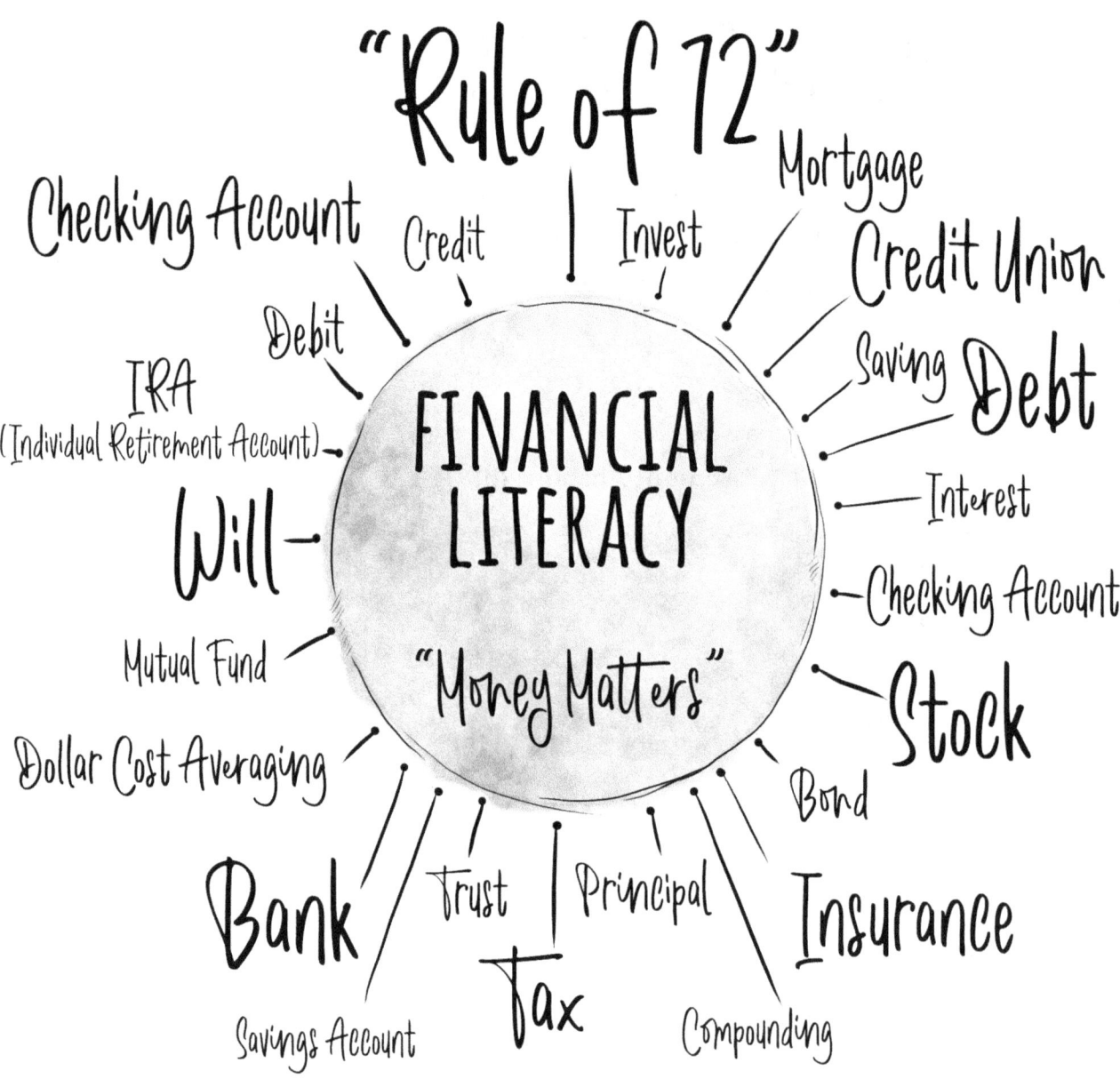

Preface
Focus: Financial Literacy

The purpose of this book is to teach youth and young adults about financial literacy, the value of money, and how money works and grows. It is meant as an introduction to teaching youth, and even young adults, about the importance and elements of saving, investing, and growing and accumulating money over time. Some of the key words, terms, or phrases include credit, debt, investing, insurance, tax, interest, principal, compounding, individual retirement accounts, stocks, mutual funds, and the "Rule of 72."

This book is meant to be a simplified version, visually engaging and stimulating, thought provoking, despite its complexity of topic, explaining how money grows over time, and the importance of saving and investing starting at an early age. It is hoped that this book will be a catalyst to propel youth to become inquisitive, motivated learners and to ask questions related to financial literacy.

This book also is for parents to evaluate, hopefully to see the book's value and provide for their son or daughter. It is hoped that they will see how this book may help their son or daughter to learn about and understand the importance of financial literacy and how it may affect their future lives.

A note from the Author:

Due to the diversity and complexity of topics and terms, from simple to complex, this book is primarily for upper elementary and middle school age students, as well as some topics for high school age and young adults. In light of the fact that most individuals in the younger age group will not yet have worked in the workplace, nor have they invested money, topics and terms used in the book are meant to familiarize these young people with real life financial literacy which will affect their lives in the future as adults.

When discussing saving and investing in this book, no specific names of companies or financial institutions are mentioned, discussed, or illustrated.

HI!
I'M MR. MELVIN
the Money Master

Another name I'm called is "Money Master Melvin." My family members include my wife, Melissa, my sons Mike and Matt, and my daughter Melanie.

Melissa

Melissa is always eager to learn how to save money. She regularly looks for reduced prices on groceries and clothing in special sales online, in magazines and newspapers, and uses reduced priced coupons for in-store purchases.

"Muscular Matt"

Matt is saving for a new exercise machine, a new set of weights, and some exercise clothing.

"Moolah Mike"

Mike does part time work to save money for things he wants, such as a new laptop and a new bicycle.

"Musical Melanie"

Melanie enjoys music and is saving for a new violin.

Malty

We also have a pesky, energetic little dog named "Malty." Malty is a Maltese dog with long, silky white fur, is very intelligent, enjoys learning new tricks, and is easy to train.

Sugar   Deb   Autumn   Scott   Norway

My special tree friends in this book are "Sugar" Maple, "Deb" Maple, "Autumn" Maple, "Scott" Pine, and "Norway" Spruce.

Northern Cardinal   American Goldfinch   Eastern Bluebird   American Robin

My special bird friends are the Northern Cardinal, American Goldfinch, Eastern Bluebird, and American Robin.

I'd like to talk to you today about money, and how important it is to save money as you earn it. Starting at an early age is really important. I'd also like to talk to you about how to make your money increase and grow over time, just as you grow bigger, older, and wiser.

This will help you to have the money you will need.

Chapter 1.
Savings and Checking Account

Money is called a **"medium of exchange."** When we purchase something, we exchange money for something we buy. When we work at a job for money, we exchange our time and labor for money we receive. In life, people work long and hard to earn money for many years. It is very important to learn about money, its value, where our money goes, how to spend it wisely, and make it grow over time.

Now I will explain and teach you some very important words or terms I would like you to know. You may know one or more of these words.

Medium of Exchange

The first word is **save**, which you probably already know. During our lifetime, we may save things we wish to keep. With money, to save is to keep or store up money for future use. The money may be saved for something special you want to buy very soon, in the near future, or distant future, something you really want to have or do. Money may be used for our future education expenses, a house, car, or a vacation.

Save

saved

Checking Account

Money may be **saved** in a **savings or checking account** in a bank or credit union. When we purchase something in a store, we may use our checking account to write a check to the store for the cost of the item. Then the store uses the check to take money out of our checking account. It is very important to have money in our checking account to cover the cost of things we buy, and to record the purchase and deduct the cost of the item from our checking account.

Savings

Certificate of Deposit

Another way to save money is to purchase a **Certificate of Deposit (CD)** at a bank or credit union. A **CD** contains an amount of money at a fixed interest rate for a fixed amount of time. A CD is safe, usually insured by the federal government. You can usually earn more money in a CD than in most savings or checking accounts, and is a way to save money for a future purchase.

Chapter 2.
Insurance

Before we go further, let's talk about **insurance**. Insurance is protection for our **assets**, things that we may own as we get older. This may include a house, car, truck, boat, jewelry, land, or other personal property. We purchase insurance coverage from an insurance company to cover expenses for loss. Property losses may be caused by storms and fires, and natural disasters such as floods, tornadoes, hurricanes, and forest fires. People may also have insurance to cover damage or theft (stealing of our property), accidents, and life insurance to cover costs when we die.

Insurance
Assets

When we get older as adults and own valuable property, we should also have a **will** which is a legal document stating who will get our property after we die. Better yet, the will and everything we own can also be put into a **living trust.** A living trust would make it easier, more efficient, and less costly to pass the property to the heirs (people who inherit another's property).

We all work very hard to earn money, to save , and invest, as well as to purchase things that we want and need. It is very important to protect what we own. If we have no will, the property will need to be administered or managed in a probate court. Even with a will, a **probate court** will need to prove that the will is authentic or valid.

Chapter 3.
TAXES

Another important term or word related to things we buy and own is **tax**. A tax is a sum of money or payment to a government (local, county, state, federal) from individuals or businesses to pay for facilities or services people use, such as schools, parks, police, library, and roads. A tax may be based upon income, sales amount, and the value of things we buy and own such as property and land.

Sales Tax

Property Taxes

When we go to the store and make purchases, we usually pay a state **sales tax** on the things that we buy. Some things in some states are tax exempt, or not taxed, such as food and clothing. When we work for someone and receive a paycheck for our work, taxes are usually taken out of our paycheck. This would include taxes going to the **state** we are working in and taxes to the **federal** government to pay for services we use and need. When we own a house or land, we must pay **property taxes** based on the value of the property.

In summary, taxes are necessary to fund the services we use and need, but have a direct effect on money that we earn to purchase, save, and invest.

State and Federal Taxes

Chapter 4.
INVEST

The next term I'd like you to know is **invest** or **investing**. To invest money is similar to saving. However, to invest money means to put money that you have earned somewhere to be able to earn more money. This money may be put into a business, buying **stocks** or **shares** of a company, or into a group of businesses called a **mutual fund.** This money may be used by a business to make more money, and your money may grow as well. A person may also invest in **bonds**. A **bond** is a certificate of ownership at a fixed interest rate, of a debt due to be paid by a government or company to an individual holder.

Stocks Shares
Invest Investing
Mutual Fund
Bonds

Savings bonds are issued by the United States Treasury Department to help pay for debt owed by the U.S. government. The most common savings bonds are I bonds and Series EE bonds. Bond holders will receive the value of the bond plus interest income when the bond is redeemed or ended. These bonds are very safe and backed by the U.S. government.

A person may choose to invest at different periods of time or on a regular basis. One way to invest is called **dollar cost averaging**. Dollar cost averaging involves deciding on an investment total to invest, then dividing the investment up into the same, smaller, regular investments, usually twice a month or monthly, over a total period of time. This method reduces risk of making one lump sum investment that is poorly timed.

Types of businesses, companies, industries large and small which we may invest in, including sectors of the economy.

Industries and sectors:

1. Technology and communication services: *(electronics, cell phones, computers, etc.)*
2. Utilities: *(electric, heating, lighting)*
3. Energy: *(renewable energy, windmills, solar panels, oil, gas)*
4. Health care: *(medical, pharmaceutical)*
5. Transportation: *(auto, airline, railroads, taxi)*
6. Food industry: *(restaurants, other)*
7. Industrials: *(things manufactured to be sold)*
8. Real estate: *(housing, commercial buildings, etc.)*
9. Financials: *(financial service companies, etc.)*
10. Agriculture: *(farm related, grain industry, agricultural coops, food producers and distributors, etc.)*

When you invest, you are putting your money to good use. You are making your money work for you and hopefully your "pot of money," meaning your money **invested**, will grow as well. Also, you may have different "pots of money" for when the money invested or saved will be used, such as for short, medium, and long term time periods. Of course, many things that you need and purchase will change as you get older.

Short Term:
new clothing, etc.

Invested

Medium Term:
new bicycle, new laptop computer, etc.

Long Term:
college, future vacation, car, something more expensive, house, etc.

Chapter 5.
Individual Retirement Account

An **Individual Retirement Account,** or **IRA**, and a **401k**, are places in which we can save and invest our money. During years when we are younger and working to earn a living, we can start putting money into an IRA and a 401k. This money is used when we are older and not working, or perhaps working part time.

IRA   Individual Retirement Account

401k

When we put money into an IRA, we can do it ourselves. One kind of IRA is a **Traditional IRA**, on which we pay taxes later. A **Roth IRA** is an IRA using money we have already paid taxes on. With a **401k**, we can have an employer or company that we are working for, do it for us. You will learn more about IRAs and 401ks as you get older and into the workforce.

Melvin can put money into an IRA by mail and direct deposit.

Melvin's company, business, or place of work automatically takes money out of his paycheck each month and putting money into his 401k.

Chapter 6.
INTEREST

The next word or term I'd like you to learn about is **interest**. You may know the word interest as something that you like or are interested in. When talking about money, interest is a sum of money, or payment, paid or charged for the use of money; that is, for borrowing someone else's money. Interest also means the rate of payment for the use of money. This rate is usually in percent.

In other words, when we borrow money, we must pay back the money we have borrowed from the lender, plus more money for using someone else's money, called interest. The interest rate may vary or change over time. A lender may be a bank, credit union, or an individual or individuals.

Example:

Mr. Melvin borrowed $1,000 from a credit union or bank to buy a new sofa. How much does he owe at the end of the year at an interest rate of 10 percent?

Start with $1,000.
Multiply $1,000 x 10% = $100 interest rate.
At the end of the year he will owe $1,100 total including principal + interest.

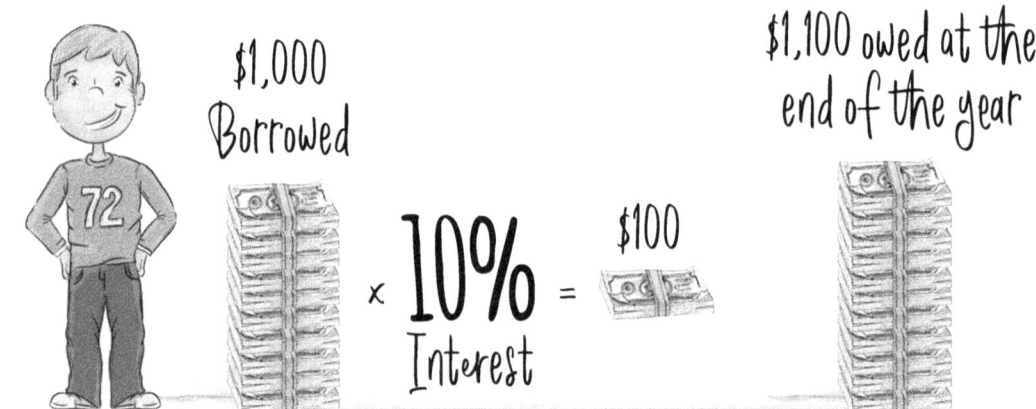

Chapter 7.
PRINCIPAL

The next word I would like you to learn is called **principal**. We are not talking about a school Principal now. When talking about money, principal is the sum of money that you start with to save or invest, not including interest or profit. The principal may increase if you continue to add to the amount of money that you save or invest. You can watch your "money pot" grow as you keep saving more and more of your money.

Principal

Watch your money pot grow as you keep saving more and more of *your money.*

Chapter 8.
COMPOUNDING

The next word or term to learn is called **compounding**. Compound means to combine two or more things, such as when two actual sentences are combined to form a compound sentence.

When talking about money, compounding means to increase or add to. That is, compounding is how money makes more money over time. To **compound** is to combine the money you are saving or investing, which is called the **principal**, plus money from **interest** that is added to that account or "pot of money" over time. Money compounds on the principal you start with plus the interest money that is added to the principal as money accumulates, or **(Principal + Interest) x Interest**. Compounding involves earning interest on your interest. The famous scientist and mathematician Albert Einstein spoke of the great importance of compounding.

Compounding

Formula Example, Year 1:

Principal: $100 to start with
Interest: 10% or .10
$100 x 10% = $10
$100 + $10 = $110 End Year 1

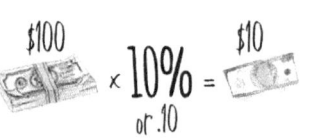
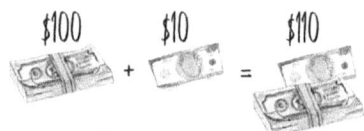

Formula Example, Year 2:

Principal: $110 to start with
Interest: 10% or .10
$110 x 10% = $11
$110 + $11 = $121 End Year 2

Formula Example, Year 3:

Principal: $121 to start with
Interest: 10% or .10
$121 x 10% = $12.10
$121 + $12.10 = $133.10 End Year 3

Chapter 9.
DEBT

The next word or term to learn is **debt**. Debt is money or something owed to someone else, to a bank or credit union, or other lender. Debt is normally not a good thing to be in. It is best to save up money to buy or purchase things that you need.

Money owed to someone else

Sometimes debt is necessary to purchase large, expensive things, such as a car, truck, or home. Then people have to borrow money from a bank, credit union, or other lending institution to purchase these things. Many people also have to go in debt and borrow money for education expenses to be able to go to a college or university.

An example of a debt on a property such as a house is called a **mortgage**. A mortgage is a deed or legal document pledging property as security for a debt. People purchase a home at a certain interest rate, which may be fixed or variable, and make payments over a certain number of years.

Chapter 10.
CREDIT

The next word or term to learn is **credit**. When talking about money, buying or purchasing on credit means agreeing to pay later for something. Credit is an amount of money owed to someone, a bank, credit union, or other lender, to be paid back at a later time. When buying on credit, we usually use a **credit card**.

Money Barrowed to be paid back later

Another card we may use is a **debit card**, from which money spent is automatically deducted from our checking account, using a PIN number.

Chapter 11.
RULE OF 72

The **"Rule of 72"** is very important. The "Rule of 72" is a method or mathematical formula to figure or calculate the approximate number of years it will take your money to double. The Rule of 72 started in 1494 with Luca Pacioli, a famous mathematician who mentioned the Rule of 72 in his book that he wrote. Some people also give credit to Albert Einstein as the individual who discovered the Rule of 72.

The "Rule of 72" will help you determine how long an investment, or debt, takes to double at a fixed interest rate on your money. As discussed before in this book, the interest rate is the amount of payment for using someone else's or another lender's money. If you have a debt that you are paying interest money on, that is not a good thing. But when you save and invest money, at a good **interest rate** which is extra money being earned, this is a good thing. Your money is compounding; that is, you are earning interest on your interest money and on the principal. Your "pot of money" is growing, at a certain interest rate, as you are growing bigger, older, and wiser.

The "Rule of 72" is a fairly simple way to determine how long an investment or debt takes to double at a fixed interest rate, using **compound interest.**

The "Rule of 72" is a **mathematical formula** that gives you the approximate number of years it will take to double your money. This is very important when we save and invest our money, and will help us to plan how much money we will have at a certain period of time. It will also help us decide how much money we should try to save regularly and over a period of time.

Formula #1, Number of years:

Number of years = 72 / Rate of Return *(or 72 divided by Rate of Return)*
The rate of return is a certain interest rate, which can vary.

Example: 72/6 = 12 years to double our money
In this example, the rate of return is 6%

Formula #2, Rate of Return:

Rate of Return = 72 / Rate of Return

Example: 72/8 = 9 years to double our money
In this example, the rate of return is 8%

Interest Rates

Now let's look at some more examples of how our money doubles at different **interest rates** when you **save** or **invest** your money. This is called **compounding**. Again, as a reminder, interest rates are based on a **percentage**, and rates vary.

The following examples will show you why it is so important to save and invest your money starting at a young age, even a small amount, if you are able, on a regular basis. Then I will provide a **compound interest table** that you can use to solve some math problems.

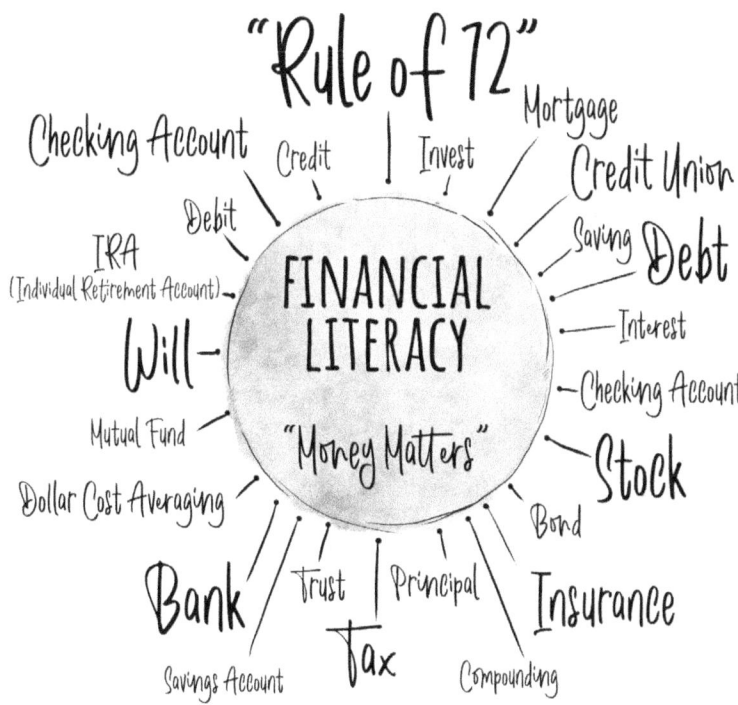

Problem example #1:

Let's say a boy, Jim, has $30. How many years will it take him to double his money at a 12% interest rate? Then he would have $60.

Solution:

Rule of 72 = 72 / 12 *(or 72 divided by 12 = 6 years)* **to double his money.**

At a 12% interest rate, Jim would then have $60 after 6 years.

12% Interest Rate

$30 — Start of Year 1

$60 — End of Year 6

Problem example #2:

Let's say a girl, Sue, also has $30. How many years will it take her money to double at a 6% interest rate? Then she would have $60.

Solution:

Rule of 72 = 72 / 6 *(or 72 divided by 6 = 12 years)* **to double her money.**

At a 6% interest rate, Sue would then have $60 after 12 years.

From these two examples, you can see that the higher the interest rate, the faster money will grow. The examples also show us how important it is to start saving and investing our money at an early age. That will allow more time for our money to grow, called **compounding**.

Another example is for money saved or invested at a 3% interest rate, that is, the rate at which your "money pot" grows in size and amount of money.

Let's say I, Mr. Melvin, have $10 to invest at a 3% interest rate. How many years will it take me to double my money, that is, for me to have twice as much money. How long would it take my "money pot" to grow twice as big?

Let's solve the problem using the **"Rule of 72."**

The Formula:

72 / 3 *(or 72 divided by 3, where 3 represents the 3 percent)*

72 / 3 = 24 years to double my money. When you divide, always put 72 on top and the number for the percentage on the bottom. So, in 24 years I would have twice as much money, or $20.

3% Interest Rate

End of 24 years

The next example is for money saved or invested at a 6% interest rate, that is, the rate at which your "money pot" grows in size and amount of money.

Let's say I, Mr. Melvin, have $10 to invest at a 6% interest rate. How many years will it take for me to double my money, that is, for me to have two times as much?

Now let's solve the problem using the **"Rule of 72."**

The Formula:

72 / 6 *(or 72 divided by 6, where 6 represents the 6 percent)*

72 / 6 = 12 years to double my money. Again, when you divide, always put 72 on top and the number for the percentage rate on the bottom. So, in 12 years I would have twice as much money, or $20. With a 6% interest rate instead of a 3% interest rate, I could double my money in 12 years instead of in 24 years, twice as fast. So, the higher the interest rate, the quicker I can double my money.

The next example is for money saved or invested at a 12% in size and amount of money. Let's say that I again have $10 to invest at a 12% interest rate. How many years will it take me, Mr. Melvin, to double my money? That is, for me to have two times or twice as much money. How long would it take me to grow twice as big?

Let's solve the problem using the **"Rule of 72."**

The Formula:

72 / 12 *(or 72 divided by 12, where 12 represents the 12 percent)*

72 / 12 = 6 years to double my money. When you divide, always put 72 on top and the number for the percentage on the bottom. So in 6 years I would have twice as much money, or $20, or be twice as big.

From the last three examples, using interest rates at 3%, 6%, and 12%, you can see that the interest rate we earn on our money is very important in how fast our money will grow.

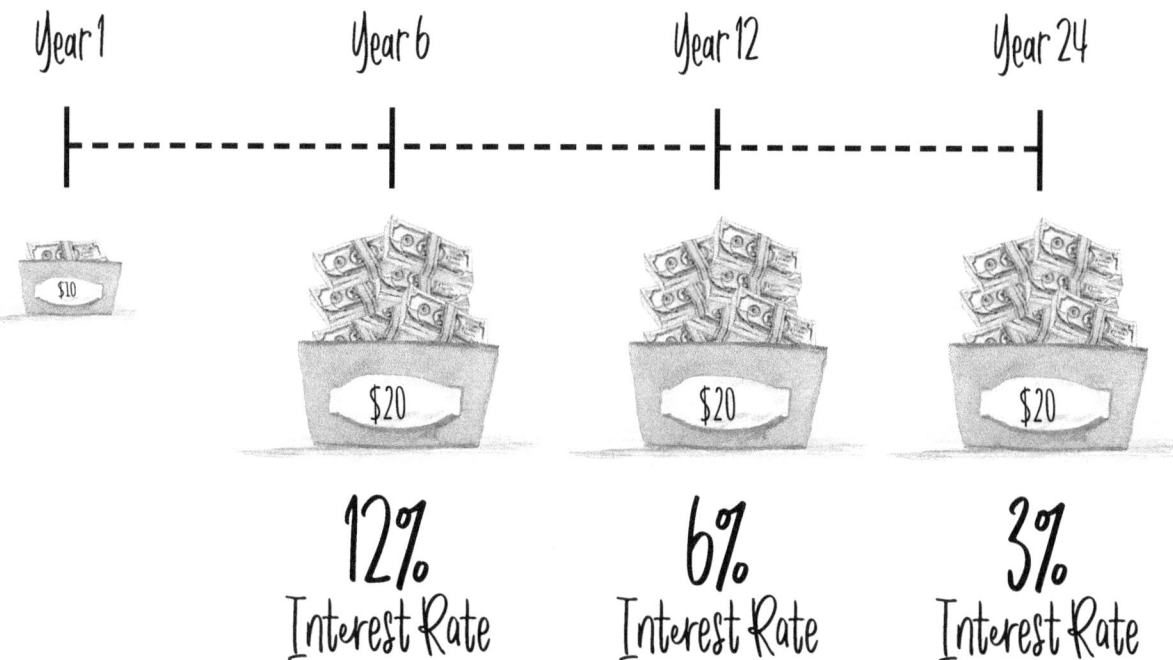

Future Money Pots Starting with $10,000 After 24 Years

3% Interest Rate — $20,000

6% Interest Rate — $40,000

12% Interest Rate — $160,000

Summary/Conclusion
Things to Remember

1. If you can, start saving early in your life when you start working. Save regularly. Make it a habit.

2. Early age saving and investing will enable your money to compound over more years and accumulate more, that is, you will have saved more money over time.

3. The interest rate on your money is very important. When you borrow money, look for the lowest interest rate. When you save money, look for the best interest rates.

4. Invest your money wisely. Get all the information that you can, learn as much as you can about saving and investing, including help and advice from professionals.

5. Study, use, and apply the Rule of 72, the approximate number of years it takes for your money to double at different interest rates.

6. Spend your money wisely. Keep track of your spending and where your money goes.

7. When getting a credit card, look for the best interest rates.

8. When spending, separate things you want from the things you need. This may help you make better decisions on what and what not to buy.

9. When saving and investing, think of "buckets" or "pots" of money for short term, medium term, and long term time periods.

I, Mr. Melvin the Money Master, and my family and friends, hope you have learned a lot about money, how money works, and how to grow and increase your money over time. Hopefully, you have learned about the importance of saving and investing money, starting at an early age if you are able to, and more as you get older as you earn money. Also, remember and apply the Rule of 72 as you save and invest.

I hope this topic of financial literacy will be a part of your lifelong learning.

MR. MELVIN

Glossary of Terms:

Bond – Certificate of ownership at a fixed interest rate of a debt due to be paid by a government or company to an individual holder, issued by the Treasury Department.

Certificate of Deposit (CD)- Amount of money purchased at a bank or credit union at a fixed interest rate for a fixed amount of time. Way to save money.

Compounding – to combine the money you are saving (Principal) plus the money that you are adding to that account based on the interest rate.

Credit – agreeing to pay later, buy on credit, using a credit card, the amount of money owed or paid to someone else at a later time.

Debt – something, or money, that is owed to someone else for a purchase.

Dollar Cost Averaging – Decide total amount to invest, invest the same, regular investments over a period of time.

Insurance – protection against loss for personal property.

Interest – rate of payment for the use of money, based on a percentage

Invest – put money that you have earned somewhere to be able to earn more money, such as money put into a company, business or businesses. Dollar cost averaging is one way to invest your money.

Mortgage - debt on a property such as a house; a deed or legal document pledging property as security for a debt.

Mutual Fund – group of companies or businesses.

Principal – the sum of money that you start with to save or invest, different from interest or profit.

Retirement Account – An account in which money is saved or invested for retirement after a person's main working years are over. Types of retirement accounts include an Individual Retirement Account (IRA) traditional (tax deferred) or Roth (tax prepaid); 401k employer sponsored retirement.

"Rule of 72" – a simple way which gives you the approximate number of years it will take to double your money; how long an investment or debt takes to double at a fixed interest rate, using compound interest. Formula: Number of years = 72/percentage rate of return using compound interest

Save – keep or store up money for future use;

Savings Account – place where money is saved, usually in a bank or credit union.

Stock – share of a company

Tax – Sum of money or payment to a government (local, county, state, federal) from individuals or businesses to pay for facilities and services people use, such as schools, parks, police, library, roads; may be based upon income, property, sales, things we buy.

Will - A legal document stating who will get property owned after we die.

"Rule of 72" – Years to Double Your Money

Worksheet 1

% Rate of Return	Years to Double Your Money Investment
1%	72 Years to double your money
2%	_____
3%	_____
4%	_____
5%	14.4
6%	_____
7%	10.28
8%	_____
9%	_____
10%	7.2
11%	6.5
12%	_____
13%	5.5
14%	5.1
15%	4.8
16%	4.5
17%	4.2
18%	_____

Worksheet 2

"Rule of 72"
Compounding of Interest and Doubling of Money

Math Problems: Figure how many years it will take your money to double, based on the Rule of 72 at each interest rate of 3%, 6%, and 12%. Divide 72 by the interest rate to solve each problem.

1. $1,000 how long would it take to double your money to $2,000
    a. _____ at 3% interest rate
    b. _____ at 6% interest rate
    c. _____ at 12% interest rate
    d. _____ at 8% interest rate
    e. _____ at 9% interest rate

2. How much money would you have if you put away/saved $10 for a certain number of years? Use the Rule of 72 Chart to answer these questions.
    a. Save $10 for 12 years at 6% interest rate _____
    b. Save $10 for 12 years at 12% interest rate _____

3. **Solve these problems.** How much money would you have at the end of the year, at a certain interest rate, starting with a set number of money? Example: Multiply the interest rate x the amount of money, then add the two figures/amounts of money together.

   Example: $100 x 3% = $3. Then add $100 + $3 = $103.00
   a. $100, 5% interest rate for one year _____
   b. $500, 5% interest rate for one year _____
   c. $500, 8% interest rate for one year _____
   d. $500, 10% interest rate for one year_____
   e. $1,000, 3% interest for one year _____
   f. $1,000, 6% interest for one year _____
   g. $1,000, 12% interest for one year_____

4. **Fill in the blanks.** The "Rule of 72" states the following:
   72 divided by the _____ _____ = the number of _____ it will take to _____ your _____.

Worksheet 3

Definitions:

Matching: Match the letter of the word or term with the proper definition using the Word Bank.

A. Compounding	H. Rule of 72	O. 401K
B. Credit	I. Certificate of Deposit (CD)	P. Insurance
C. Debt	J. Save	Q. Stock
D. Interest	K. Tax	R. Mortgage
E. IRA	L. Savings Account	S. Mutual Fund
F. Invest	M. Roth	T. Will
G. Principal	N. Bond	

1. ____ Method used to show the approximate number of years it will take to double your money.

2. ____ Keep or store up money for future use.

3. ____ Sum of money you start with to save or invest.

4. ____ Individual Retirement Account

5. ____ Protection for our personal property against loss

6. ____ Share of a company

7. ____ Money that is owed to someone else.

8. ____ Sum of money or payment to a government from individuals or businesses to pay for facilities, schools, parks, police, and other services.

9. _____ Rate of payment for the use of money, based on a percentage.

10. _____ Retirement account set up with an employer (someone you work for) to save or put away money.

11. _____ Agreement to pay later.

12. _____ Group of companies or businesses

13. _____ Combine money you are saving (principal) plus the money that is being added to the account based on the interest rate:
(principal + interest) x Interest

14. _____ A type of Individual Retirement Account (IRA) that is used after taxes have already been paid for on money to be put into the account.

15. _____ Account in which money is saved, usually in a bank or credit union.

16. _____ Deed or legal document pledging property as security for a debt; debt on a property such as a house.

17. _____ Put money that you have earned somewhere to be able to earn more money, such as money put into a business, businesses, or companies.

18. _____ Certificate of ownership at a fixed interest rate of a debt due to be paid by a government or company to an individual holder.

19. _____ Way to save money. Amount of money purchased at a bank or credit union at a fixed interest rate for a fixed amount of time.

20. _____ Is a legal document stating who will get our property after we die.

Worksheet 4

Financial Literacy
Discussion Questions

1. What does financial literacy mean to you? Explain why it is important to learn about financial literacy.

2. What are some important things about money or things related to money you learned about from reading this book?

3. Why is it important to start saving and investing money, if you are able to, at an early age instead of when you are older? How may it affect you when you are perhaps retired or not working?

4. What is the definition and formula for the Rule of 72? Why is it important to know about the Rule of 72? Give or write down an example using the Rule of 72.

5. What is compounding of money? What is the formula or equation for compounding of money? How does money work and earn more money over time? Why is it very important?

6. What does IRA stand for? How will an IRA benefit people when they are older and perhaps retired from work?

7. What is insurance? Why do we need insurance? What are some things we protect with insurance? How may insurance or not having it affect the money that we may have?

8. What are taxes? How do taxes affect the money that we have or earn? Why are taxes necessary? What some things we pay taxes for? Where does the money go?

9. What is interest? How can interest help us, or increase our money? ? How can interest hurt us, or decrease our money?

10. What is debt? How can debt be a bad thing? When is debt usually necessary? What are some things a person may need to go into debt for to be able to buy? How do people get into debt? How can debt affect our lives?

Worksheet 4

The Rule of 72

The Rule of 72 demonstrates the approximate number of years to double your money, at a fixed interest rate, using compound interest.

Formula:
72 / Interest Rate = Years to Double Your Money

The table on the next page shows how the Rule of 72 works and is an approximation of total dollars accumulated. Rates of return may fluctuate on some investments, and the table is not intended to represent these specific types of investments.

Number of Years	3%	6%	9%	12%
0 years	$10,000	$10,000	$10,000	$10,000
6 years				$20,000
8 years			$20,000	
12 years		$20,000		$40,000
16 years			$40,000	
18 years				$80,000
24 years	$20,000	$40,000	$80,000	$160,000
30 years				$320,000
32 years			$160,000	
36 years		$80,000		$640,000

About the Author

Roger F. Hartwich Jr., M.S.E., M.S., B.S., B.A., has been a school teacher and a landscaper/landscape designer/horticulturist/arborist for many years. Roger has taught full time K-12 Special Education, regular elementary education, and most subject areas, including German, as a K-12 substitute teacher. Roger has owned a landscaping company for many years, and worked in financial services for a short period of time. Roger has strong interest in environmental preservation, trees, horticulture, arboriculture, and landscape design as well as financial literacy.

Roger is an Army veteran and former Navy Reservist, Navy Reserve Retired, with 20 years of military service. Roger holds Masters Degrees in Special Education and Recreation and Park Administration, a B.S. Degree in Elementary Education, a B.A. Degree in Social Science, German minor, and a technical college degree in horticulture/landscape technology and design.

Roger believes in relating and applying learning to real life skills. He has special interest in financial literacy. He sees a strong need in school and society for providing more financial literacy for youth and young adults. He has written this book for youth and young adults in general, as well as for interested parents who desire to have their sons and daughters well-grounded in financial literacy and provided with financial literacy information and literature.

Roger currently resides in Wisconsin.

www.ingramcontent.com/pod-product-compliance
Lightning Source LLC
Chambersburg PA
CBHW080036120526
44589CB00036B/2623